THE BIG BOOK OF

ALEXANDER POPE

POPE

QUOTES

Curated by M.K.

"The greatest magnifying glasses in the world are a man's own eyes when they look upon his own person."

"Fools rush in where angels fear to tread."

"A little learning is a dangerous thing; Drink deep, or taste not the Pierian spring."

.

"To err is human; to forgive, divine."

"In faith and hope the world will disagree, but all mankind's concern is charity."

"Teach me to feel another's woe, to hide the fault I see, that mercy I to others show, that mercy show to me."

"The best way to prove the clearness of our mind, is by showing its faults; as when a stream discovers the dirt at the bottom, it convinces us of the transparency and purity of the water."

"Chiefs who no more in bloody fights engage, But wise through time, and narrative with age, In summer-days like grasshoppers rejoice - A bloodless race, that send a feeble voice."

"While pensive poets painful vigils keep, Sleepless themselves, to give their readers sleep."

"See! From the brake the whirring pheasant springs,
And mounts exulting on triumphant wings;
Short is his joy! He feels the fiery wound,
Flutters in blood, and panting beats the ground."

"To the Elysian shades dismiss my soul, where no carnation fades."

"Genius creates, and taste preserves."

"No louder shrieks to pitying heaven are cast, When husbands or lap-dogs breathe their last."

"Satire's my weapon, but I'm too discreet To run amuck, and tilt at all I meet."

"No one should be ashamed to admit they are wrong, which is but saying, in other words, that they are wiser today than they were yesterday."

"Seas roll to waft me, suns to light me rise; My footstool earth, my canopy the skies."

"A little learning is a dangerous thing."

"But see, Orion sheds unwholesome dews; Arise, the pines a noxious shade diffuse; Sharp Boreas blows, and nature feels decay, Time conquers all, and we must time obey."

"Every woman is at heart a rake."

"Modest plainness sets off sprightly wit,
For works may have more with than does 'em good,
As bodies perish through excess of blood."

"The most positive men are the most credulous, since they most believe themselves, and advise most with their falsest flatterer and worst enemy-their own self-love."

"Our plenteous streams a various race supply, The bright-eyed perch with fins of Tyrian dye, The silver eel, in shining volumes roll'd, The yellow carp, in scales bedropp'd with gold, Swift trouts, diversified with crimson stains, And pikes, the tyrants of the wat'ry plains."

"Now hollow fires burn out to
black,
And lights are fluttering low:
Square your shoulders, lift your
pack
And leave your friends and go.
O never fear, lads, naught's to dread,
Look not to left nor right:
In all the endless road you tread
There's nothing but the night."

"Strength of mind is exercise, not rest."

"To be angry is to revenge the faults of others on ourselves."

"On life's vast ocean diversely we sail. Reasons the card, but passion the gale."

"Of all the causes which conspire to blind Man's erring judgement, and misguide the mind, What the weak head with strongest bias rules, Is PRIDE, the never-failing vice of fools."

"Act well your part, there all the honour lies."

"Monuments, like men, submit to fate."

"He who tells a lie is not sensible of how great a task he undertakes; for he must be forced to invent twenty more to maintain that one."

"O peace! how many wars were
waged in thy name."

"At every trifle take offense, that always shows great pride or little sense."

"Hills peep o'er hills, and Alps on
Alps arise."

"Say, will the falcon, stooping from above, Smit with her varying plumage, spare the dove? Admires the jay the insect's gilded wings? Or hears the hawk when Philomela sings?"

"Love the offender, yet detest the offense."

"A tree is a nobler object than a prince in his coronation-robes."

"Some people will never learn anything, for this reason, because they understand everything too soon."

"True wit is nature to advantage dressed;
What oft was thought, but ne'er so well expressed."

"A brain of feathers, and a heart of lead."

"All are but parts of one stupendous whole, Whose body Nature is, and God the soul."

"Do good by stealth, and blush to find it fame."

"The only time you run out of
chances is when you stop taking
them."

"The ruling passion, be it what it will. The ruling passion conquers reason still."

"How shall I lose the sin, yet keep the sense, and love the offender, yet detest the offence?"

"Soft is the strain when zephyr
gently blows."

"A pear-tree planted nigh:
'Twas charg'd with fruit that made a
goodly show,
And hung with dangling pears was
every bough."

"And soften'd sounds along the waters die: Smooth flow the waves, the zephyrs gently play."

"Calm, thinking villains, whom no faith could fix, Of crooked counsels and dark politics."

"Then marble, soften'd into life,
grew warm."

"Never elated when someone's oppressed, never dejected when another one's blessed."

"A little learning is a dangerous thing; drink of it deeply, or taste it not, for shallow thoughts intoxicate the brain, and drinking deeply sobers us again."

"On wrongs swift vengeance waits."

"Charm strikes the sight, but merit wins the soul."

"Blessed is the man who expects nothing, for he shall never be disappointed was the ninth beatitude."

"Remembrance and reflection how allied. What thin partitions divides sense from thought."

"All seems infected that th' infected spy,
As all looks yellow to the jaundiced eye."

"What then remains, but well our
power to use,
And keep good-humor still whate'er
we lose?
And trust me, dear, good-humor
can prevail,
When airs, and flights, and screams,
and scolding fail."

"Nature and nature's laws lay hid in the night. God said, Let Newton be! and all was light!"

"Fools admire, but men of sense approve."

"An excuse is worse and more terrible than a lie; for an excuse is a lie guarded."

"Search then the ruling passion; there alone, The wild are constant, and the cunning known; The fool consistent, and the false sincere; Priests, princes, women, no dissemblers here."

"The difference is as great between The optics seeing as the objects seen. All manners take a tincture from our own; Or come discolor'd through out passions shown; Or fancy's beam enlarges, multiplies, Contracts, inverts, and gives ten thousand dyes."

"In men, we various ruling passions find; In women, two almost divide the kind Those, only fixed, they first or last obey, The love of pleasure, and the love of sway."

"Lo! the poor Indian! whose
untutor'd mind
Sees God in clouds, or hears him in
the wind;
His soul proud Science never taught
to stray
Far as the solar walk or milky way."

"Genius creates, and taste preserves. Taste is the good sense of genius; without taste, genius is only sublime folly."

"I am his Highness' dog at Kew;
Pray tell me, sir, whose dog are
you?"

"What dire offence from am'rous causes springs, What mighty contests rise from trivial things."

"The difference is too nice - Where ends the virtue or begins the vice."

"He who serves his brother best gets nearer God than all the rest."

"Luxurious lobster-nights, farewell,
For sober, studious days!"

"Soft o'er the shrouds aerial whispers breathe, That seemed but zephyrs to the train beneath."

"The lights and shades, whose well-accorded strife gives all the strength and color of our life."

"What is it to be wise?
'Tis but to know how little can be
known,
To see all others' faults, and feel our
own."

"Religion blushing, veils her sacred fires, And unawares Morality expires."

"By flatterers besieged And so obliging that he ne'er obliged."

"Light quirks of music, broken and uneven,Make the soul dance upon a jig to Heav'n."

"He best can paint them who shall feel them most."

"Nothing can be more shocking and horrid than one of our kitchens sprinkled with blood, and abounding with the cries of expiring victims or with the limbs of dead animals scattered or hung up here and there."

"Many men have been capable of doing a wise thing, more a cunning thing, but very few a generous thing."

"Beauties in vain their pretty eyes may roll; charms strike the sight, but merit wins the soul."

"A person who is too nice an observer of the business of the crowd, like one who is too curious in observing the labor of bees, will often be stung for his curiosity."

"What some call health, if purchased by perpetual anxiety about diet, isn't much better than tedious disease."

"Order is heaven's first law."

"A work of art that contains theories is like an object on which the price tag has been left."

"Lo! The poor Indian, whose untutored mind sees God in clouds, or hears him in the wind."

"Music resembles poetry, in each
Are nameless graces which no
methods teach, And which a master
hand alone can reach."

"All looks yellow to a jaundiced eye."

"If, presume not to God to scan; The proper study of Mankind is Man. Plac'd on this isthmus of a middle state, a being darkly wise, and rudely great."

"The Physician, by the study and inspection of urine and ordure, approves himself in the science; and in like sort should our author accustom and exercise his imagination upon the dregs of nature."

"Expression is the dress of thought, and still Appears more decent as more suitable; A vile conceit in pompous words express'd, Is like a clown in regal purple dress'd."

"Rogues in rags are kept in
countenance by rogues in ruffles."

"There never was any party, faction, sect, or cabal whatsoever, in which the most ignorant were not the most violent; for a bee is not a busier animal than a blockhead."

"Genius involves both envy and calumny."

"See plastic Nature working to this end, The single atoms each to other tend, Attract, attracted to, the next in place Form'd and impell'd its neighbor to embrace."

"Love, free as air, at sight of human ties,
Spreads his light wings, and in a moment flies."

"The sound must seem an echo to the sense."

"Most women have no characters at all."

"See how the World its Veterans
rewards!
A Youth of Frolics, an old Age of
Cards;
Fair to no purpose, artful to no end,
Young without Lovers, old without
a Friend;
A Fop their Passion, but their Prize
a Sot;
Alive ridiculous, and dead forgot."

"Our judgments, like our watches,
none go just alike, yet each believes
his own."

"An honest man's the noblest work
of God."

"Education forms the common mind. Just as the twig is bent, the tree's inclined."

"The most positive men are the most credulous."

"Chaos of thought and passion, all confused; Still by himself abused or disabused; Created half to rise, and half to fall; Great lord of all things, yet a prey to all; Sole judge of truth, in endless error hurled,- The glory, jest, and riddle of the world."

"You eat, in dreams, the custard of the day."

"Not always actions show the man; we find who does a kindness is not therefore kind."

"Unthought-of Frailties cheat us in the Wise."

"Fortune in men has some small
diff'rence made,
One flaunts in rags, one flutters in
brocade,
The cobbler apron'd, and the parson
gown'd,
The friar hooded, and the monarch
crown'd."

"As the twig is bent, so grows the tree."

"Amusement is the happiness of those who cannot think."

"Every professional was once an amateur."

"'Tis thus the mercury of man is fix'd, Strong grows the virtue with his nature mix'd."

"Pleas'd look forward, pleas'd to look behind, And count each birthday with a grateful mind."

"Conceit is to nature what paint is to beauty; it is not only needless, but it impairs what it would improve."

"As with narrow-necked bottles; the less they have in them, the more noise they make in pouring out."

"Happy the man whose wish and care a few paternal acres bound, content to breathe his native air in his own ground."

"Histories are more full of examples of the fidelity of dogs than of friends."

"Praise undeserved, is satire in disguise."

"The way of the Creative works through change and transformation, so that each thing receives its true nature and destiny and comes into permanent accord with the Great Harmony: this is what furthers and what perseveres."

"They dream in courtship, but in wedlock wake."

"This long disease, my life."

"Love seldom haunts the breast
where learning lies,
And Venus sets ere Mercury can
rise."

"Be silent always when you doubt
your sense."

"Order is Heaven's first law; and this confess, Some are and must be greater than the rest."

"Envy will merit as its shade pursue,
But like a shadow, proves the substance true."

"Whate'er the talents, or howe'er designed, We hang one jingling padlock on the mind."

"There is a majesty in simplicity."

"Learning is like mercury, one of
the most powerful and excellent
things in the world in skillful hands;
in unskillful, the most mischievous."

"T]hro? this Air, this Ocean, and this Earth, All Nature quick, and bursting into birth. Above, how high progressive life may go? Around how wide? how deep extend below? Vast Chain of Being! which from God began, Ethereal Essence, Spirit, Substance, Man, Beast, Bird, Fish, Insect! what no Eye can see, No Glass can reach! from Infinite to Thee! From Thee to Nothing. From Nature?s Chain whatever Link you strike, Tenth, or ten thousandth, breaks the chain alike. All are but parts of one stupendous Whole: Whose Body Nature is, and God the Soul."

"True politeness consists in being easy one's self, and in making every one about one as easy as one can."

"The world forgetting, by the world forgot. Eternal sunshine of the spotless mind! Each pray'r accepted, and each wish resign'd."

"Sole judge of Truth, in endless Error hurled: / The glory, jest, and riddle of the world!"

"Women use lovers as they do cards; they play with them a while, and when they have got all they can by them, throw them away, call for new ones, and then perhaps lose by the new all they got by the old ones."

"And more than echoes talk along the walls."

.

"Aurora now, fair daughter of the dawn, Sprinkled with rosy light the dewy lawn."

"Who dare to love their country,
and be poor."

"Lend, lend your wings! I mount! I fly!
O grave! where is thy victory?
O death! where is thy sting?"

"Wine works the heart up, wakes the wit,
There is no cure 'gainst age but it."

"Coffee which makes the politician
wise, and see through all things
with his half-shut eyes."

"You purchase pain with all that joy can give and die of nothing but a rage to live."

"But blind to former as to future fate, what mortal knows his pre-existent state?"

"Men must be taught as if you taught them not, and things unknown proposed as things forgot."

"For forms of government, let fools contest; Whate'er is best administered, is best."

"It is very natural for a young friend and a young lover to think the persons they love have nothing to do but to please them."

"Sleep and death, two twins of winged race,
Of matchless swiftness, but of silent pace."

"A king may be a tool, a thing of straw; but if he serves to frighten our enemies, and secure our property, it is well enough; a scarecrow is a thing of straw, but it protects the corn."

"I begin where most people end, with a full conviction of the emptiness of all sorts of ambition, and the unsatisfactory nature of all human pleasures."

"Let fortune do her worst, whatever she makes us lose, so long as she never makes us lose our honesty and our independence."

"But Satan now is wiser than of yore, and tempts by making rich, not making poor."

"True ease in writing comes from art, not chance, As those move easiest who have learned to dance."

"Those move easiest who have learn'd to dance."

"Our passions are like convulsion fits, which, though they make us stronger for a time, leave us the weaker ever after."

"There is a certain majesty in simplicity which is far above all the quaintness of wit."

"And all who told it added something new, and all who heard it, made enlargements too."

"Know then thyself, presume not God to scan; The proper study of mankind is man."

"Lo, what huge heaps of littleness around!"

"Drink is the feast of reason and the flow of soul."

"Condition, circumstance, is not the thing; Bliss is the same in subject or in king."

"From vulgar bounds with brave disorder part, And snatch a grace beyond the reach of art."

"Ye flowers that drop, forsaken by
the spring,
Ye birds that, left by summer, cease
to sing,
Ye trees that fade, when Autumn
heats remove,
Say, is not absence death to those
who love?"

"Whether with Reason, or with Instinct blest, Know, all enjoy that pow'r which suits them best."

"The time shall come, when, free as seas or wind, Unbounded Thames shall flow for all mankind, Whole nations enter with each swelling tide, And seas but join the regions they divide; Earth's distant ends our glory shall behold, And the new world launch forth to seek the old."

"Reason, however able, cool at best,
Cares not for service, or but serves
when prest, Stays till we call, and
then not often near."

"With sharpen'd sight pale Antiquaries pore, Th' inscription value, but the rust adore. This the blue varnish, that the green endears; The sacred rust of twice ten hundred years."

"Good sense, which only is the gift of Heaven, And though no science, fairly worth the seven."

"Choose a firm cloud before it fall,
and in it Catch, ere she change, the
Cynthia of this minute."

"For what I have publish'd, I can only hope to be pardon'd; but for what I have burned, I deserve to be prais'd."

"That character in conversation which commonly passes for agreeable is made up of civility and falsehood."

"On cold December fragrant chaplets blow, And heavy harvests nod beneath the snow."

"Alas! the small discredit of a bribe
Scarce hurts the lawyer, but undoes
the scribe."

.

"Be niggards of advice on no pretense; For the worst avarice is that of sense."

"The Right Divine of Kings to
govern wrong."

"Then, at the last and only couplet fraught With some unmeaning thing they call a thought, A needless Alexandrine ends the song, That, like a wounded snake, drags its slow length along."

"Beauty draws us with a single hair."

"The vanity of human life is like a river, constantly passing away, and yet constantly coming on."

"Dear, damned, distracting town, farewell! Thy fools no more I'll tease: This year in peace, ye critics, dwell, Ye harlots, sleep at ease!"

"Thou wert my guide, philosopher, and friend."

"Is not absence death to those who love?"

"Sickness is a sort of early old age; it teaches us a diffidence in our earthly state."

"Every man has just as much vanity
as he wants understanding."

"Superstition is the spleen of the soul."

"New, distant Scenes of endless Science rise: So pleas'd at first, the towring Alps we try."

"Is there a parson much bemused in beer, a maudlin poetess, a rhyming peer, a clerk foredoom'd his father's soul to cross, who pens a stanza when he should engross?"

"Some praise at morning what they blame at night, but always think the last opinion right."

"Statesman, yet friend to truth! of soul sincere, In action faithful, and in honour clear; Who broke no promise, serv'd no private end, Who gain'd no title, and who lost no friend."

"Sure of their qualities and demanding praise, more go to ruined fortunes than are raised."

"What Reason weaves, by Passion is undone."

"Pride is still aiming at the best houses: Men would be angels, angels would be gods. Aspiring to be gods, if angels fell; aspiring to be angels men rebel."

"False happiness is like false money; it passes for a time as well as the true, and serves some ordinary occasions; but when it is brought to the touch, we find the lightness and alloy, and feel the loss."

"Behold the child, by Nature's kindly law pleased with a rattle, tickled with a straw."

"Not to go back is somewhat to advance, and men must walk, at least, before they dance."

"All nature is but art unknown to thee."

"The proper study of Mankind is Man."

"No woman ever hates a man for being in love with her, but many a woman hate a man for being a friend to her."

"Hope springs eternal in the human breast: Man never is, but always To be Blest."

"For critics, as they are birds of prey, have ever a natural inclination to carrion."

"To swear is neither brave, polite, nor wise."

"The laughers are a majority."

"Wholesome solitude, the nurse of sense!"

"No craving void left aching in the soul."

"And empty heads console with
empty sound."

"There is but one way I know of conversing safely with all men; that is, not by concealing what we say or do, but by saying or doing nothing that deserves to be concealed."

"What Tully said of war may be applied to disputing: "It should be always so managed as to remember that the only true end of it is peace. " But generally true disputants are like true sportsmen,-their whole delight is in the pursuit; and the disputant no more cares for the truth than the sportsman for the hare."

"By music minds an equal temper know,
Nor swell too high, nor sink too low.
.
Warriors she fires with animated sounds.
Pours balm into the bleeding lover's wounds."

"For forms of faith let graceless zealots fight; his can't be wrong whose life is in the right."

"Never elated while one man's oppress'd;
Never dejected while another's blessed."

"So upright Quakers please both man and God."

"There should be, methinks, as little merit in loving a woman for her beauty as in loving a man for his prosperity; both being equally subject to change."

"Ask for what end the heavenly
bodies shine,
Earth for whose use? Pride answers,
'Tis for mine
For me kind nature wakes her
genial power,
Suckles each herb, and spreads out
every flower."

"Who are next to knaves? Those that converse with them."

"Honor and shame from no condition rise. Act well your part: there all the honor lies."

"So vast is art, so narrow human wit."

"Trust not yourself, but your defects to know, make use of every friend and every foe."

"A wit with dunces, and a dunce with wits."

"Wit is the lowest form of humor."

"Health consists with temperance
alone."

"Tis but a part we see, and not a whole."

"Of Manners gentle, of Affections mild; In Wit a man; Simplicity, a child."

"Never find fault with the absent."

"Gentle dullness ever loves a joke."

"Like Cato, give his little senate laws, and sit attentive to his own applause."

"One science only will one genius fit; so vast is art, so narrow human wit."

"Our rural ancestors, with little blest, Patient of labor when the end was rest, Indulged the day that housed their annual grain, With feasts, and off'rings, and a thankful strain."

"Good-nature and good-sense must
ever join;
To err is human, to forgive, divine."

"The vulgar boil, the learned roast,
an egg."

"Virtue she finds too painful an
endeavour, content to dwell in
decencies for ever."

"And seem to walk on wings, and
tread in air."

"True disputants are like true sportsmen: their whole delight is in the pursuit."

"The spider's touch, how exquisitely fine!
Feels at each thread, and lives along the line."

"We think our fathers fools, so wise we grow. Our wiser sons, no doubt will think us so."

"Here am I, dying of a hundred good symptoms."

"Did some more sober critics come abroad? If wrong, I smil'd; if right, I kiss'd the rod."

"An obstinate person does not hold opinions; they hold them."

"In this commonplace world every one is said to be romantic who either admires a fine thing or does one."

"Passions are the gales of life."

"Fondly we think we honor merit
then, when we but praise ourselves
in other men."

"Astrologers that future fates
foreshow."

"Education forms the common mind."

"For lo! the board with cups and spoons is crowned. The berries crackle, and the mill turns round . At once they gratify their scent and taste. And frequent cups prolong the rich repast. Coffee (which makes the politician wise And see through all things with his half-shut eyes)."

"As some to Church repair, not for
the doctrine, but the music there."

"A king is a mortal god on earth, unto whom the living God hath lent his own name as a great honour; but withal told him, he should die like a man, lest he should be proud, and flatter himself that God hath with his name imparted unto him his nature also. JOHN LOCKE, "Of a King", The Conduct of the Understanding: Essays, Moral, Economical, and Political A king may be a tool, a thing of straw; but if he serves to frighten our enemies, and secure our property, it is well enough: a scarecrow is a thing of straw, but it protects the corn."

"Fame can never make us lie down contentedly on a deathbed."

.

"Nothing is more certain than much of the force; as well as grace, of arguments or instructions depends their conciseness."

"See the wild Waste of all-devouring years! How Rome her own sad Sepulchre appears, With nodding arches, broken temples spread! The very Tombs now vanish'd like their dead!"

"In pride, in reas'ning pride, our error lies; All quit their sphere and rush into the skies. Pride still is aiming at the bless'd abodes, Men would be angels, angels would be gods."

"Then sculpture and her sister arts revived; stones leaped to form, and rocks began to live."

"And not a vanity is given in vain."

"But would you sing, and rival Orpheus' strain. The wond'ring forests soon should dance again; The moving mountains hear the powerful call. And headlong streams hand listening in their fall!"

"Offend her, and she knows not to forgive; Oblige her, and she'll hate you while you live."

"Of darkness visible so much be lent, as half to show, half veil, the deep intent."

"But just disease to luxury succeeds,
And ev'ry death its own avenger
breeds."

"And little eagles wave their wings
in gold."

"How glowing guilt exalts the keen delight!"

"No more the mounting larks, while Daphne sings, Shall, list'ning, in mid-air suspend their wings."

"Great oaks grow from little acorns. He has a green thumb. He has green fingers. He's sowing his wild oats. Here Ceres' gifts in waving prospect stand, And nodding tempt the joyful reaper's hand."

"All chance, direction, which thou canst not see."

"Love finds an altar for forbidden fires."

"Ask you what provocation I have had? The strong antipathy of good to bad."

"Most authors steal their works, or buy."

"To endeavor to work upon the vulgar with fine sense is like attempting to hew blocks with a razor."

"We may see the small value God has for riches, by the people he gives them to."

"Where beams of imagination play, the memory's soft figures melt away."

"Where grows?-where grows it not?
If vain our toil, We ought to blame
the culture, not the soil."

"Oh, sons of earth! attempt ye still to rise. By mountains pil'd on mountains to the skies? Heav'n still with laughter the vain toil surveys, And buries madmen in the heaps they raise."

"Judges and senates have been bought for gold; Esteem and love were never to be sold."

"Hear how the birds, on ev'ry blooming spray, With joyous musick wake the dawning day."

"Our proper bliss depends on what
we blame."

"For wit and judgment often are at strife, Though meant each other's aid, like man and wife."

"Learn of the little nautilus to sail,
Spread the thin oar, and catch the
driving gale."

"Of fight or fly, This choice is left ye, to resist or die."

"Who know but He, whose hand the lightning forms, Who heaves old ocean, and who wings the storms, Pours fierce ambition in a Caesar's mind."

"Judge not of actions by their mere effect; Dive to the center, and the cause detect. Great deeds from meanest springs may take their course, And smallest virtues from a mighty source."

"A long, exact, and serious comedy; In every scene some moral let it teach, And, if it can, at once both please and preach."

"There still remains to mortify a wit
The many-headed monster of the
pit."

"Unblemish'd let me live or die unknown; Oh, grant an honest fame, or grant me none!"

"To dazzle let the vain design, To raise the thought and touch the heart, be thine!"

"The soul, uneasy and confin'd from home, Rests and expatiates in a life to come."

"What Conscience dictates to be done, Or warns me not to do; This teach me more than Hell to shun, That more than Heav'n pursue."

"The mouse that always trusts to one poor hole Can never be a mouse of any soul."

"In adamantine chains shall Death be bound, And Hell's grim tyrant feel th' eternal wound."

"Dogs, ye have had your day!"

"I was not born for courts and great affairs, but I pay my debts, believe and say my prayers."

"There goes a saying, and 'twas shrewdly said, "Old fish at table, but young flesh in bed."

"Fine sense and exalted sense are not half so useful as common sense."

"A family is but too often a commonwealth of malignants."

"With too much quickness ever to be taught; With too much thinking to have common thought."

"Our business in the field of fight, Is not to question, but to prove our might."

"A good-natured man has the whole
world to be happy out of."

"Order is Heaven's first law; and this confessed, some are, and must be, greater than the rest, more rich, more wise; but who infers from hence that such are happier, shocks all common sense. Condition, circumstance, is not the thing; bliss is the same in subject or in king."

"In the nice bee, what sense so
subtly true
From pois'nous herbs extracts the
healing dew?"

"I as little fear that God will damn a man that has charity, as I hope that the priests can save one who has not."

"Tis not a lip, or eye, we beauty call,
But the joint force and full result of
all."

"Search then the ruling passion:
This clue, once found, unravels all
the rest."

"Some are bewildered in the maze of schools, And some made coxcombs nature meant but fools."

"Truth needs not flowers of speech."

"Now warm in love, now with'ring
in my bloom Lost in a convent's
solitary gloom!"

"Be thou the first true merit to befriend, his praise is lost who stays till all commend."

"Envy will merit, as its shade, pursue."

"All looks yellow to a jaundiced eye that habitually compares everything to something better. But by changing that habit to comparing everything to something worse, even making it a game, that person can find gratitude, relief and happiness where-ever they go and whatever they experience, guaranteed!"

"And write about it, Goddess, and about it!"

"An atheist is but a mad, ridiculous derider of piety, but a hypocrite makes a sober jest of God and religion; he finds it easier to be upon his knees than to rise to a good action."

"The young disease, that must subdue at length, Grows with his growth, and strengthens with his strength."

"Eye Nature's walks, shoot folly as it flies, And catch the manners living as they rise; Laugh where we must, be candid where we can, But vindicate the ways of God to man."

"Awake, my St. John! leave all meaner things To low ambition and the pride of kings. Let us (since life can little more supply Than just to look about us, and to die) Expatiate free o'er all this scene of man; A mighty maze! but not without a plan."

"Reason's whole pleasure, all the joys of sense, Lie in three words,-health, peace, and competence."

"Pleased to the last, he crops the flowery food, And licks the hand just raised to shed his blood."

"Wretches hang that jurymen may dine."

"On wings of wind came flying all abroad."

"For I, who hold sage Homer's rule the best, Welcome the coming, speed the going guest."

"But honest instinct comes a volunteer; Sure never to o'er-shoot, but just to hit, While still too wide or short in human wit."

"While I live, no rich or noble knave shall walk the world in credit to his grave."

"Th' unwilling gratitude of base mankind!"

"Grave authors say, and witty poets sing, That honest wedlock is a glorious thing."

"Learn from the beasts the physic of the field."

"So modern 'pothecaries, taught the art By doctor's bills to play the doctor's part, Bold in the practice of mistaken rules, Prescribe, apply, and call their masters fools."

"Live like yourself, was soon my lady's word, And lo! two puddings smok'd upon the board."

"At length corruption, like a general flood (So long by watchful ministers withstood), Shall deluge all; and avarice, creeping on, Spread like a low-born mist, and blot the sun."

"The doubtful beam long nods from side to side."

"Envy, to which th' ignoble mind's a slave, Is emulation in the learn'd or brave."

"Some positive persisting fops we know, Who, if once wrong, will needs be always so; But you with pleasure own your errors past, And make each day a critique on the last."

"Pretty! in amber to observe the forms Of hairs, of straws, or dirt, or grubs, or worms! The things, we know, are neither rich nor rare, But wonder how the devil they got there."

"Heaven forming each on other to depend, A master, or a servant, or a friend, Bids each on other for assistance call, Till one man's weakness grows the strength of all."

"What riches give us let us then inquire: Meat, fire, and clothes. What more? Meat, clothes, and fire. Is this too little?"

"The hog that ploughs not, not obeys thy call, Lives on the labours of this lord of all."

"The approach of night The skies yet blushing with departing light, When falling dews with spangles deck'd the glade, And the low sun had lengthen'd ev'ry shade."

"See Christians, Jews, one heavy sabbath keep, And all the western world believe and sleep."

"To what base ends, and by what abject ways, Are mortals urg'd through sacred lust of praise!"

"Satire or sense, alas! Can Sporus feel? Who breaks a butterfly upon a wheel?"

"Age and want sit smiling at the gate."

"What is fame? a fancied life in others' breath."

"When two people compliment each other with the choice of anything, each of them generally gets that which he likes least."

"Avoid Extremes; and shun the fault of such Who still are pleas'd too little or too much."

"Nor in the critic let the man be lost."

"The Muse but serv'd to ease some friend, not wife, / To help me through this long disease, my life."

"I have more zeal than wit."

"Poets heap virtues, painters gems, at will, And show their zeal, and hide their want of skill."

"Silence! coeval with eternity! thou wert ere Nature's self began to be; thine was the sway ere heaven was formed on earth, ere fruitful thought conceived creation's birth."

"No creature smarts so little as a fool."

"Give me again my hollow tree A crust of bread, and liberty!"

"The man that loves and laughs
must sure do well."

"A man who admires a fine woman, has yet not more reason to wish himself her husband, than one who admired the Hesperian fruit, would have had to wish himself the dragon that kept it."

"Vast chain of being! which from God began, Natures ethereal, human, angel, man, Beast, bird, fish, insect, what no eye can see, No glass can reach, from infinite to Thee, From Thee to nothing."

"In a sadly pleasing strain, let the warbling lute complain."

"But see how oft ambition's aims are cross'd, and chiefs contend 'til all the prize is lost!"

"Mark what unvary'd laws preserve each state, Laws wise as Nature, and as fixed as Fate."

"When to mischief mortals bend their will, how soon they find it instruments of ill."

"Tis strange the miser should his cares employTo gain those riches he can ne'er enjoy;Is it less strange the prodigal should wasteHis wealth to purchase what he ne'er can taste?"

"First follow Nature, and your
judgment frame
By her just standard, which is still
the same:
Unerring nature, still divinely
bright,
One clear, unchanged, and universal
light,
Life, force, and beauty must to all
impart,
At once the source, and end, and
test of art."

"Nor Fame I slight, nor for her favors call; She comes unlooked for, if she comes at all ."

"What bosom beast not in his country's cause?"

"But thousands die without or this or that, Die, and endow a college or a cat."

"Heaven from all creatures hides the book of Fate."

"Ye gods, annihilate but space and time,
And make two lovers happy."

"Ah! what avails it me the flocks to keep,
Who lost my heart while I preserv'd my sheep."

"The scripture in times of disputes is like an open town in times of war, which serves in differently the occasions of both parties."

"Of all affliction taught a lover yet,
'Tis true the hardest science to
forget."

"Know, Nature's children all divide her care, The fur that warms a monarch warmed a bear."

"Who sees with equal eye, as God of all, A hero perish or a sparrow fall, Atoms or systems into ruin hurl'd, And now a bubble burst, and now a world."

"True friendship's laws are by this rule express'd,
Welcome the coming, speed the parting guest."

"Placed on this isthmus of a middle
state,
A being darkly wise and rudely
great.
He hangs between; in doubt to act
or rest;
In doubt to deem himself a god, or
beast;
In doubt his mind or body to prefer;
Born to die, and reasoning but to
err."

"When much dispute has past, we find our tenets just the same as last."

"A brave man thinks no one his superior who does him an injury, for he has it then in his power to make himself superior to the other by forgiving it."

"A generous friendship no cold medium knows, Burns with one love, with one resentment glows."

"Consult the genius of the place, that paints as you plant, and as you work."

"Is that a birthday? 'tis, alas! too clear; 'Tis but the funeral of the former year."

.

"Blest paper-credit! last and best supply! That lends corruption lighter wings to fly!"

"What's fame? a fancy'd life in other's breath. A thing beyond us, even before our death."

"Find, if you can, in what you cannot change. Manners with fortunes, humours turn with climes, Tenets with books, and principles with times."

"To rest, the cushion and soft dean invite, who never mentions hell to ears polite."

"A brave man struggling in the storms of fate, And greatly falling with a falling state."

"Let sinful bachelors their woes deplore; full well they merit all they feel, and more: unaw by precepts, human or divine, like birds and beasts, promiscuously they join."

"In lazy apathy let stoics boast, their virtue fixed, 'tis fixed as in a frost."

"See skulking Truth to her old cavern fled, Mountains of Casuistry heap'd o'er her head! Philosophy, that lean'd on Heav'n before, Shrinks to her second cause, and is no more. Physic of Metaphysic begs defence, And Metaphysic calls for aid on Sense! See Mystery to Mathematics fly!"

"Fly, dotard, fly! With thy wise dreams and fables of the sky."

"Absent or dead, still let a friend be dear."

"Such labour'd nothings, in so strange a style, Amaze th' unlearn'd and make the learned smile."

"Chaste to her husband, frank to all beside, A teeming mistress, but a barren bride."

"Oft, as in airy rings they skim the heath, The clamtrous lapwings feel the leaden death; Oft, as the mounting larks their notes prepare They fall, and leave their little lives in air."

"The worst of madmen is a saint run mad."

"To observations which ourselves we make, we grow more partial for th' observer's sake."

"Party-spirit at best is but the madness of many for the gain of a few."

"The same ambition can destroy or save, and make a patriot as it makes a knave."

"All Nature is but art, unknown to thee All chance, direction, which thou canst not see; All discord, harmony not understood; All partial evil, universal good."

"Ambition first sprung from your blest abodes: the glorious fault of angels and of gods."

"Know then this truth, enough for man to know virtue alone is happiness below."

"Tis not enough your counsel still be true; Blunt truths more mischief than nice falsehoods do."

"Vice is a monster of so frightful mien As to be hated needs but to be seen; Yet seen too oft, familiar with her face, We first endure, then pity, then embrace."

"Some old men, continually praise the time of their youth. In fact, you would almost think that there were no fools in their days, but unluckily they themselves are left as an example."

"The bookful blockhead, ignorantly read With loads of learned lumber in his head."

"Woman's at best a contradiction still."

"The hungry judges soon the sentence sign, and wretches hang that jurymen may dine."

"Extremes in nature equal ends
produce; In man they join to some
mysterious use."

"Men would be angels, angels would be gods."

"Hope travels through, nor quits us
when we die."

"A God without dominion, providence, and final causes, is nothing else but fate and nature."

"Is pride, the never-failing vice of fools."

"Who shall decide when doctors disagree, And soundest casuists doubt, like you and me?"

"How happy is the blameless vestal's lot? The world forgetting, by the world forgot."

"Lulled in the countless chambers of the brain, our thoughts are linked by many a hidden chain; awake but one, and in, what myriads rise!"

"Ten censure wrong for one who writes amiss."

"Oh! if to dance all night, and dress
all day,
Charm'd the small-pox, or chas'd
old age away;

.

To patch, nay ogle, might become a
saint,
Nor could it sure be such a sin to
paint."

"Pride, where wit fails, steps in to our defence, and fills up all the mighty void of sense."

"Thus unlamented pass the proud away,
The gaze of fools and pageant of a day;
So perish all, whose breast ne'er learn'd to glow
For others' good, or melt at others' woe."

"Pleasure, or wrong or rightly understood,
Our greatest evil, or our greatest good."

"But touch me, and no minister so
sore.
Whoe'er offends, at some unlucky
time
Slides into verse, and hitches in a
rhyme,
Sacred to ridicule his whole life
long,
And the sad burthen of some merry
song."

"All nature mourns, the skies relent
in showers; hushed are the birds,
and closed the drooping flowers."

"There is nothing wanting to make all rational and disinterested people in the world of one religion, but that they should talk together every day."

"And hence one master-passion in the breast, Like Aaron's serpent, swallows up the rest."

"What so pure, which envious
tongues will spare?
Some wicked wits have libell'd all
the fair,
With matchless impudence they
style a wife,
The dear-bought curse, and lawful
plague of life;
A bosom serpent, a domestic evil,
A night invasion, and a mid-day
devil;
Let not the wise these sland'rous
words regard,
But curse the bones of ev'ry living
bard."

"Heaven gave to woman the
peculiar grace
To spin, to weep, and cully human
race."

"Our grandsire, Adam, ere of Eve
possesst,
Alone, and e'en in Paradise unblest,
With mournful looks the blissful
scenes survey'd,
And wander'd in the solitary shade.
The Maker say, took pity, and
bestow'd
Woman, the last, the best reserv'd
of God."

"Ladies, like variegated tulips, show
'Tis to their changes half their
charms we owe."

"Talk what you will of taste, my friend, you'll find two of a face as soon as of a mind."

"Taste, that eternal wanderer, which flies
From head to ears, and now from ears to eyes."

"It is sure the hardest science to forget!"

"The search of our future being is but a needless, anxious, and haste to be knowing, sooner than we can, what, without all this solicitude, we shall know a little later."

"True self-love and social are the same."

"The dull flat falsehood serves for policy, and in the cunning, truth's itself a lie."

"A field of glory is a field for all."

"Such as are still observing upon others are like those who are always abroad at other men's houses, reforming everything there while their own runs to ruin."

"Homer excels all the inventors of other arts in this: that he has swallowed up the honor of those who succeeded him."

"The life of a wit is a warfare upon earth."

"Wit and judgment often are at strife."

"Count all th' advantage prosperous Vice attains,
'Tis but what Virtue flies from and disdains:
And grant the bad what happiness they would,
One they must want-which is, to pass for good."

"Sometimes virtue starves while vice is fed."

"Virtue may choose the high or low degree,
'Tis just alike to virtue, and to me;
Dwell in a monk, or light upon a king,
She's still the same belov'd, contented thing."

"Court-virtues bear, like gems, the highest rate,
Born where Heav'n influence scarce can penetrate.
In life's low vale, the soil the virtues like,
They please as beauties, here as wonders strike."

"O let us still the secret joy partake,
To follow virtue even for virtue's
sake."

"Intestine war no more our passions wage,
And giddy factions bear away their rage."

"Behold the groves that shine with silver frost, their beauty withered, and their verdure lost!"

"Go, wiser thou! and in thy scale of sense weigh thy opinion against Providence."

"A fellow feeling makes us
wondrous kind."

"Fickle Fortune reigns, and, undiscerning, scatters crowns and chains."

"Music the fiercest grief can charm,
And fate's severest rage disarm.
Music can soften pain to ease,
And make despair and madness
please;
Our joys below it can improve,
And antedate the bliss above."

"The villain's censure is extorted praise."

"One self-approving hour whole
years outweighs."

"The character of covetousness, is what a man generally acquires more through some niggardliness or ill grace in little and inconsiderable things, than in expenses of any consequence."

"Mankind is unamendable."

"Old politicians chew on wisdom
past,
And totter on in business to the
last."

"That each from other differs, first confess; next that he varies from himself no less."

"A youth of frolic, an old age of cards."

"What will a child learn sooner than
a song?"

"Authors, like coins, grow dear as they grow old."

"Some place the bliss in action, some in ease,
Those call it pleasure, and contentment these."

"Pleasures are ever in our hands or eyes;
And when in act they cease, in prospect rise."

"The greatest advantage I know of being thought a wit by the world is, that it gives one the greater freedom of playing the fool."

"If a man's character is to be abused there's nobody like a relative to do the business."

"I find myself hoping a total end of all the unhappy divisions of mankind by party-spirit, which at best is but the madness of many for the gain of a few."

"And die of nothing but a rage to live."

"At ev'ry word a reputation dies."

"Words are like Leaves; and where they most abound, Much Fruit of Sense beneath is rarely found."

"Nor public flame, nor private, dares to shine; Nor human spark is left, nor glimpse divine! Lo! thy dread empire, Chaos! is restored; Light dies before thy uncreating word: Thy hand, great Anarch! lets the curtain fall; And universal darkness buries all."

"How vast a memory has Love!"

"She went from opera, park, assembly, play,
To morning walks, and prayers three hours a day.
To part her time 'twixt reading and bohea,
To muse, and spill her solitary tea,
Or o'er cold coffee trifle with the spoon,
Count the slow clock, and dine exact at noon."

"Fix'd like a plant on his peculiar
spot,
To draw nutrition, propagate and
rot."

"Time conquers all, and we must time obey."

"Fair tresses man's imperial race ensnare; And beauty draws us with a single hair."

"Virtuous and vicious every man must be, few in the extreme, but all in the degree."

"I believe it is no wrong Observation, that Persons of Genius, and those who are most capable of Art, are always fond of Nature, as such are chiefly sensible, that all Art consists in the Imitation and Study of Nature. On the contrary, People of the common Level of Understanding are principally delighted with the Little Niceties and Fantastical Operations of Art, and constantly think that finest which is least Natural."

"Here thou, great Anna! Whom three realms obey, / Dost sometimes counsel take—and sometimes tea."

"To happy convents, bosomed deep
in vines,
Where slumber abbots, purple as
their wines."

"Good God! how often are we to die before we go quite off this stage? In every friend we lose a part of ourselves, and the best part."

"Two purposes in human nature rule. Self- love to urge, and reason to restrain."

"Why has not Man a microscopic eye? For this plain reason, Man is not a Fly. Say what the use, were finer optics giv'n, T' inspect a mite, not comprehend the heav'n."

"O happiness! our being's end and
aim!
Good, pleasure, ease, content!
whate'er thy name:
That something still which prompts
the eternal sigh,
For which we bear to live, or dare
to die."

"Whenever I find a great deal of gratitude in a poor man, I take it for granted there would be as much generosity if he were a rich man."

"But see, the shepherds shun the
noonday heat,
The lowing herds to murmuring
brooks retreat,
To closer shades the panting flocks
remove;
Ye gods! And is there no relief for
love?"

"Where'er you walk cool gales shall fan the glade, Trees where you sit shall crowd into a shade. Where'er you tread the blushing flowers shall rise, And all things flourish where you turn your eyes."

"Praise from a friend, or censure
from a foe, Are lost on hearers that
our merits know."

"Get place and wealth, if possible with grace; if not, by any means get wealth and place."

"He knows to live who keeps the middle state, and neither leans on this side nor on that."

"To balance Fortune by a just expense, Join with Economy, Magnificence."

"It often happens that those are the best people whose characters have been most injured by slanderers: as we usually find that to be the sweetest fruit which the birds have been picking at."

"But to the world no bugbear is so great, As want of figure and a small estate."

"Do you find yourself making excuses when you do not perform? Shed the excuses and face reality. Excuses are the loser's way out. They will mar your credibility and stunt your personal growth."

"E'en Sunday shines no Sabbath day
to me."

"Fool, 'tis in vain from wit to wit to roam: Know, sense, like charity, begins at home."

"Destroy all creatures for thy sport
or gust, Yet cry, if man's unhappy,
God's unjust."

"Who finds not Providence all good and wise, Alike in what it gives, and what denies."

"In various talk th' instructive hours they past, Who gave the ball, or paid the visit last; One speaks the glory of the British queen, And one describes a charming Indian screen; A third interprets motions, looks, and eyes; At every word a reputation dies."

"Oh! blest with temper, whose unclouded ray Can make to-morrow cheerful as to-day."

"Who pants for glory, finds but short repose; A breath revives him, or a breath o'erthrows."

"What nature wants, commodious gold bestows; 'Tis thus we cut the bread another sows."

"Not half so swift the trembling doves can fly, When the fierce eagle cleaves the liquid sky; Not half so swiftly the fierce eagle moves, When thro' the clouds he drives the trembling doves."

"Others import yet nobler arts from France, Teach kings to fiddle, and make senates dance."

"And bear about the mockery of woe To midnight dances and the public show."

"Thus let me live, unseen, unknown, Thus unlamented let me die, Steal from the world, and not a stone Tell where I lie."

"On her white breast a sparkling cross she wore, Which Jews might kiss and infidels adore."

"But thinks, admitted to that equal sky, His faithful dog shall bear him company."

"The dances ended, all the fairy train For pinks and daisies search'd the flow'ry plain."

"Tis true, 'tis certain; man, though dead, retains Part of himself; the immortal mind remains."

"Some judge of authors' names, not works, and then Nor praise nor blame the writings, but the men."

"The nicest constitutions of government are often like the finest pieces of clock-work, which, depending on so many motions, are therefore more subject to be out of order."

"Get your enemy to read your works in order to mend them, for your friend is so much your second self that he will judge too like you."

"I never knew any man in my life who could not bear another's misfortunes perfectly like a Christian."

"Wine lets no lover unrewarded go."

"To be, contents his natural desire,
He asks no angel's wing, no seraph's
fire;
But thinks, admitted to that equal
sky,
His faithful dog shall bear him
company.
Go wiser thou! and in thy scale of
sense
Weigh thy opinion against
Providence."

"And each blasphemer quite escape
the rod, Because the insult's not on
man, but God?"

"What can ennoble sots, or slaves, or cowards? Alas! not all the blood, of all the Howards."

"The blest to-day is as completely
so, As who began a thousand years
ago."

"No Senses stronger than his brain can bear. Why has not Man a microscopic eye? For this plain reason, Man is not a Fly: What the advantage, if his finer eyes Study a Mite, not comprehend the Skies?. Or quick Effluvia darting thro' his brain, Die of a Rose, in Aromatic pain? If Nature thunder'd in his opening ears, And stunn'd him with the music of the Spheres. Who finds not Providence all-good and wise, Alike in what it gives, and what denies?"

Made in the USA
Columbia, SC
01 November 2024

7809c870-bd6a-4929-a8b7-b0cf2aed85ecR01